On a
Plane

Experts on child reading levels
have consulted on the level of text and
concepts in this book.

At the end of the book is a "Look Back and Find" section
which provides additional information and encourages
the child to refer back to previous pages
for the answers to the questions posed.

Angela Grunsell trained as a teacher in 1969.
She has a Diploma in Reading and Related Skills
and for the last five years has advised London
teachers on materials and resources.
She works for the ILEA as an advisory teacher in
primary schools in Hackney, London.

Published in the United States in 1984 by
Franklin Watts, 387 Park Avenue South, New York, NY 10016

© Aladdin Books Ltd/Franklin Watts

Designed and produced by
Aladdin Books Ltd, 70 Old Compton Street, London W1

ISBN 0-531-04716-4

Printed in Belgium

FRANKLIN · WATTS · FIRST · LIBRARY

On a Plane

by
Kate Petty

Consultant
Angela Grunsell

Illustrated by
Aline Riquier

Franklin Watts
London · New York · Toronto · Sydney

Do you want to fly in a plane?
What is it like?

Hundreds of planes fly to and from
this airport every day.
They can take you all over the world.

At the check-in desk an attendant looks
at your ticket and checks your bags.
How much does the suitcase weigh?

The bags are labeled so that
they won't get lost.
Then they are taken away and
loaded onto the plane.

You show your passport and go through
security control into the departure lounge.
You wait here until your flight is called.

"Flight 901 to London now boarding at Gate 3."
That's your flight.
The plane is ready to go.

As the plane taxis to the runway the stewardess makes sure that everyone is comfortable. Have you fastened your seat belt for takeoff?

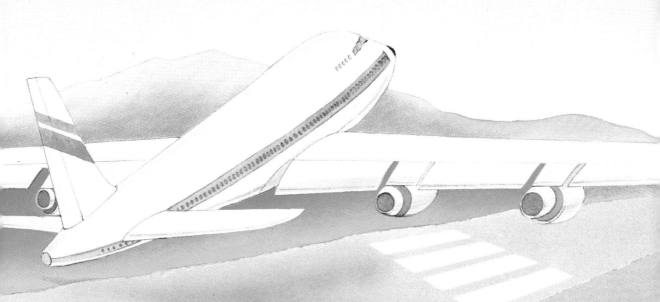

The engines roar at full power
as the plane rushes up the runway.
Suddenly you have left the ground.

The plane rises through the clouds
like an enormous bird.
The powerful engines keep it moving forward
but it is the specially shaped wings that
keep the plane in the air.

The clouds look like
masses of cotton.
Far below you can see
tiny fields and towns.

15

Now the stewardesses and stewards have to work very hard. They have to serve lunch to three hundred passengers.

Can you see how the food is served?
After lunch you can watch a movie

You have been invited up to the flight deck
where the pilots are. It is very bright
and you can see for miles around.

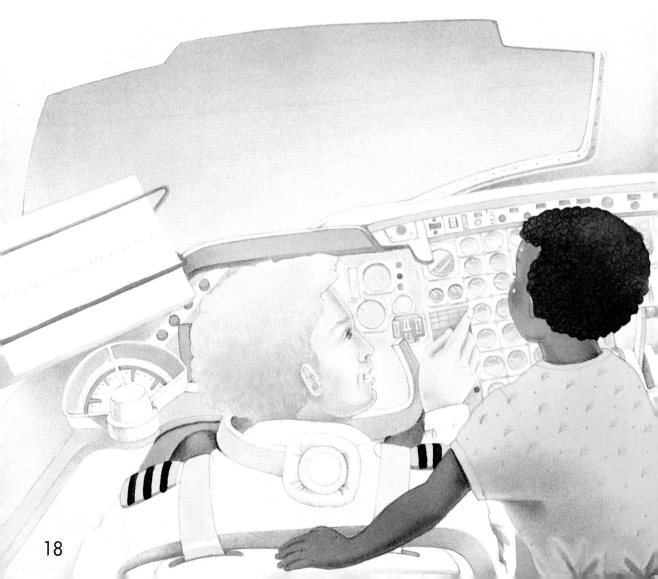

The pilot shows you how fast and how high you are traveling. He uses his radar system to keep away from other planes.

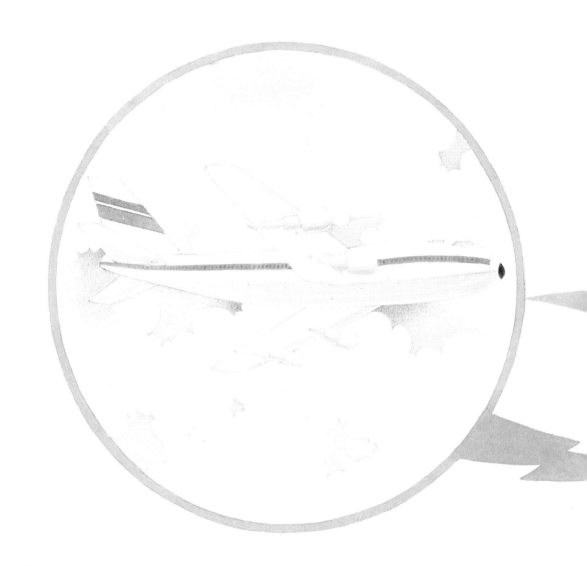

The flight is nearly over.
The pilot contacts the control tower
at the busy airport so that he can be told
when it is his turn to land.

The air traffic controllers watch
all the planes coming in on radar screens.
They radio instructions to the pilot.

Fasten your seat belt. You're coming down.
Your ears feel funny so you swallow hard.
Soon you can make out houses and cars
on the streets below.

Did you hear the wheels being lowered?
You feel a slight jolt as you touch down.
The engines roar, the brakes go on
and the plane slows down.

You've arrived. In just nine hours you have come a quarter of the way around the world. By boat it would have taken about two weeks.

Before you leave the airport you must collect your bags and go through customs. Can you see your bags on the carousel?

A huge crowd is waiting to meet passengers from many different places. The arrivals board tells them which planes have landed.

Suddenly you see your friends waving.
You can't wait to tell them
what it was like on the plane.

XU	251	TOKYO	12 40
BA	828	BAHRAIN	12 55
KL	469	AMSTERDAM	13 15
BW	901	BARBADOS	13 30

AI	427	MILAN
LT	955	FRANKFUR

Look back and find

What does the attendant at the
check-in desk do?

Why are the bags weighed?
*The pilot needs to know exactly how much
weight he is carrying to take off safely.*

What happens at security.control?
*A metal detector makes sure no one
is carrying a gun or a bomb.*

How do you know when your flight
is ready to go?

When must you wear a seat belt?
*For takeoff and landing and sometimes
during the flight if it gets bumpy.*

What must the plane do before
it leaves the ground?
*It needs to gather lots of speed
to be able to take off.*

How high and how fast does a plane
usually fly?
*About 6.2 miles (10,000 m) high at a speed of
558 miles (900 km) per hour.*
How does the pilot know his height and speed?
He reads from the dials in the flight deck.

What else does he use?

Why does the pilot contact
the control tower when he wants to land?

What happens when several planes want to
land at the same time?
*They fly in circles, one above the other,
over the airport. This is called stacking.
They move down as the lowest plane lands.*

Why do your ears feel funny as the plane
starts to land?
*Your body always reacts to a rapid change in
height. It can also happen to you in elevators.*

Why do the engines roar?
*They are put into reverse thrust
to slow the plane down.*

Index

PRINTED IN BELGIUM BY

INTERNATIONAL BOOK PRODUCTION